Table of Contents

Reference[1] - U.S. Department of Justice FBI: A Study of Active Shooter Incidents in the United States Between 2000 and 2013

Active Shooter Definition

Active Shooter (AS) events have tragically become a routine part of our news media diet. By steadily digesting these incidents, the term Active Shooter has become a household term. However, this term often gets misapplied to situations that are tragic, but are not truly Active Shooter incidents. So what is an Active Shooter event?

The definition provided by United States Homeland Security[1] is "an individual actively engaged in killing or attempting to kill people in a confined and populated area." This definition points out the two keys that differentiate Active Shooter events from other situations.

1)Actively Engaged
2)Confined and Populated Area

Actively Engaged – This is not a situation where a person has gone into a bank and taken hostages. It involves much  more than a "threat". These incidents are distinguished by the fact that the suspect is *actively* taking lives, or *actively* attempting to take them.

Confined and Populated Area – The term Active Shooter could not be properly applied to a person that burglarizes a home and gets in a confrontation with the homeowners. Even if such a situation ended in fatality, it does not meet the criteria of being a heavily populated area.

Why does it matter that we define what an Active Shooter is? The events are heartbreaking whether they are isolated or on a large scale. Does the definition really make a difference? YES!

The term Active Shooter has been used by law enforcement to describe a situation that is in progress. The key to this is that the definition of this event will affect protocols and responses at the scene. It should also be noted that while the term Active Shooter is most commonly applied to incidents involving firearms (shooting), the term can and has been applied to incidents involving other weapons. Active Shooter protocols are enacted when the two prongs are met:

1) Actively Engaged
2) Confined and Populated Area

So if you are not a member of law enforcement, how does it benefit you to understand the definition of Active Shooter? These events are different than other crimes. The term *active* inherently implies that **both** citizens and law enforcement personnel have the potential to affect the outcome of such an event based upon their responses.

Active Shooter Locations

Where do Active Shooter events take place? The FBI did a comprehensive study in 2014. They examined Active Shooter incidents that occurred between 2000 and 2013[1]. They determined that out of 160 cases the following approximate percentages applied:

- 45% - Mall or Business
- 25% - Schools
- 10% - Government Facility
- 20% - Miscellaneous Locations (Churches, Hospitals, Etc.)

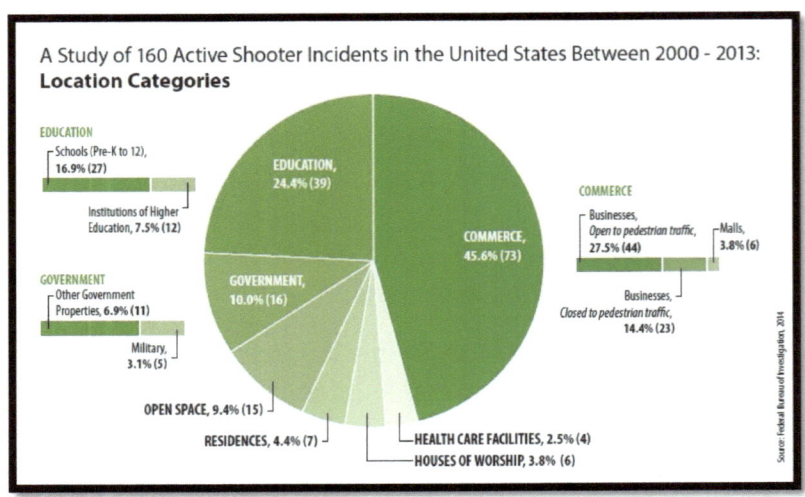

A Study of 160 Active Shooter Incidents in the United States Between 2000 - 2013: **Location Categories**

EDUCATION
Schools (Pre-K to 12), 16.9% (27)
Institutions of Higher Education, 7.5% (12)

EDUCATION, 24.4% (39)

COMMERCE
Businesses, Open to pedestrian traffic, 27.5% (44)
Malls, 3.8% (6)
Businesses, Closed to pedestrian traffic, 14.4% (23)

COMMERCE, 45.6% (73)

GOVERNMENT
Other Government Properties, 6.9% (11)

GOVERNMENT, 10.0% (16)

Military, 3.1% (5)

OPEN SPACE, 9.4% (15)

RESIDENCES, 4.4% (7)

HEALTH CARE FACILITIES, 2.5% (4)

HOUSES OF WORSHIP, 3.8% (6)

Source: Federal Bureau of Investigation, 2014

Active Shooter Frequency

Perhaps you have heard the news about a few recent Active Shooter incidents. Maybe they were not in an area that you are intimately familiar with, or have family in. In such a situation, it is easy to find yourself thinking "these events are fairly uncommon". It can be easy to fool ourselves into believing these are rare occurrences that will never affect us. Below is a breakdown of the number of Active Shooter episodes in the U.S. by year.

2000	1	2005	9	2010	26
2001	6	2006	10	2011	10
2002	4	2007	14	2012	21
2003	11	2008	8	2013	17
2004	4	2009	19	2014	20

By adding the 20 Active Shooter cases that occurred in 2014 to the 160 previously listed by U.S. Homeland Security from 2000 to 2013[1], we get a total of 180 incidents in 15 years. This leaves us with the following chilling statistics on frequency of occurrence:

☉ 6.4 / Annual Occurrences (2000 – 2006)
☉ 16.88 / Annual Occurrences (2007 – 2014)

As you can see, the number of these events has nearly tripled. So even if you have not been personally touched by an Active Shooter incident, chances are steadily increasing that you will be.

6

Active Shooter Casualties

What has fueled this phenomenon that we know as Active Shooter? Many experts agree that the driving force behind the majority of these attacks is notoriety of some sort. Sometimes this is the result of feeling "picked on" or being treated like an "outcast" by others. In some cases, it is the desire to bring the spotlight to a particular cause or belief held by the offender.

How does this type of action bring attention? Sadly, it can be summed up in two words; body count. Persons

 contemplating undertaking such disturbing actions have seen that the more carnage they can cause, the more media coverage they will receive. This direct correlation has motivated them to find unique and morbid ways of increasing the death toll in a single incident.

For some, this means bringing more weapons with them. For others it means using other equipment, such as chains and locks, to prevent their would-be victims from escaping. Recently, we have seen attackers seeking out places that are highly populated and confined, which had not previously been thought of as potential "targets" for these types of assaults. The results from these incidents that occurred between 2000 and 2013 are listed below:

- ☺ 557 Wounded
- ☺ 486 Killed
- ☺ 1,043 Total Casualties

*The attackers are not included in these figures

Active Shooter Conclusions

When Active Shooter events begin, many believe that they should simply do their best to hide and wait for law enforcement to arrive. The average person does not believe it is up to them to handle such a situation. They choose to wait for those that are professionally trained in such matters to arrive on scene. Does this rationale make sense?

When we examine the 160 incidents that the FBI studied, the results are shocking. In a little over 50% of these cases, law enforcement responded in 10 minutes or less. While this might frighten you to learn, that is statistically a very good, and quite commendable, response time. The problem is that almost 70% of these events concluded in less than 5 minutes. In fact, 35% of these incidents lasted less than 2 minutes. This means that even with a very desirable response time, law enforcement is statistically going to arrive *after* the event has already concluded.

There is a 75% chance that an Active Shooter incident will be concluded by one of the following:

1. Citizen Engagement
2. Shooter's Choice

The FBI printed this conclusion in their 2014 study[1], "Even when law enforcement was present or able to respond within minutes, civilians often had to make life and death decisions, and, therefore, should be engaged in training and discussions on decisions they may face."

Active Shooter Preparation

What can you do to prepare yourself for such a catastrophic event? Some people do not like to think about such a terrible situation. Many choose to overlook the crucial aspect of planning for a tragic event such as an Active Shooter.

Earthquakes can be horrific events, especially in areas that are susceptible to having them. How can loss of life be minimized in such areas? Such situations require planning in order to minimize the devastating impact. Would it make sense to ignore such a threat and fail to properly prepare for it because it is terrifying? Of course not.

It should be noted that most schools in the United States have emergency drills that are practiced with the students. These include; fire drills, earthquake drills, and Active Shooter drills. Why do schools practice such drills?

The answer is simple; studies show that rehearsing a situation *before* it occurs, dramatically affects your ability to have a successful outcome. Sports psychologists have performed experiments that show basketball players who repeatedly practice making free-throws, by seeing the event in their minds, are statistically just as good, if not better, than the player that practices free-throws physically. Mental rehearsal is important in sports, but it is even more crucial when it comes to your safety.

This is why law enforcement officers are trained to handle life-threatening situations in a sterile training environment. Going through "worst-case scenario" drills helps their brains to be better prepared to react. By repeating these drills, situations that seem to unfold at lightning speed, suddenly begin to slow down. Sound decisions are easier to make under these circumstances.

Think back to when you first learned to drive a car. Initially, you no doubt felt anxiety as you maneuvered the vehicle at slow speeds. Entering traffic was extremely stressful as you learned how to perform the necessary skills required in driving.

Now think about your first time driving on the freeway. Do you remember how intimidating it was to see vehicles moving so fast all around you? But with practice, things began to slow down in your brain. Now you may find yourself driving down the freeway,  changing songs on your stereo, talking to your passenger and sipping your coffee…all simultaneously.

Did the traffic slow down to make this possible? No, your repeated practice and experience at driving caused the events to slow down in your mind. Things were no longer as overwhelming to your brain. This in turn allowed your brain to be free to work on other tasks at hand. In fact, your brain is now performing the driving tasks in auto-pilot mode.

The same is true when it comes to preparing yourself for an Active Shooter situation. You should not create a single plan for yourself, you should have *multiple* plans to help your brain work through potential scenarios.

To mentally prepare yourself for such a terrible situation takes courage and mental fortitude. But the results can ultimately save your life, and the lives of those around you. Maintaining rational thought under the stress of an irrational situation is the key. How can you train your brain to remain calm?

Active Shooter preparation has three key elements, the ABC's:

- ✒ A – Assessment
- ✒ B – Battle
- ✒ C – Conclusion

Preparation ABC's
A – Assessment

Assessment – You should take note of any areas you may find yourself in that could be likely locations of an Active Shooter attack.

Remember what an Active Shooter situation is comprised of; an individual actively engaged in killing or attempting to kill people in a *confined* and *populated* area. What confined and populated areas do you find yourself in; your church, school, place of business, shopping centers?

Once you have identified locations where you could potentially find yourself in an Active Shooter situation, think about precautions you could take. Are you aware of the nearest exits at these locations? What areas could potentially be good hiding spots? Are there locking doors that you could use to protect yourself?

Once you have identified these potential items that can be used for your safety, begin to mentally rehearse. Play out some scenarios in your mind as you walk through the mall. What would you do if you saw somebody coming down the corridor shooting a gun? Could you run outside from your current location? Could you find a secure hiding spot?

What about at work? Envision yourself performing your normal tasks. What would you do if a disgruntled former employee burst into your work area and began shooting? Would there be an area to run or hide? Would it place you in such close proximity that you would be forced to fight?

Now try to create your own scenarios. Remember that this is by no means an easy exercise. But the goal of this is to help your brain start learning to identify safe steps that you can take in *any* situation. You are trying to slow things down for your brain, just like driving on the freeway. Eventually, your brain will learn to analyze such things in auto-pilot mode.

Just as you have learned through repetitive practice to perform dangerous maneuvers on auto-pilot, mental rehearsal of scenarios can help you to make sound decisions under stress.

Preparation ABC's
B – Battle

Battle – Be prepared to make split-second decisions under the stress of an Active Shooter incident.

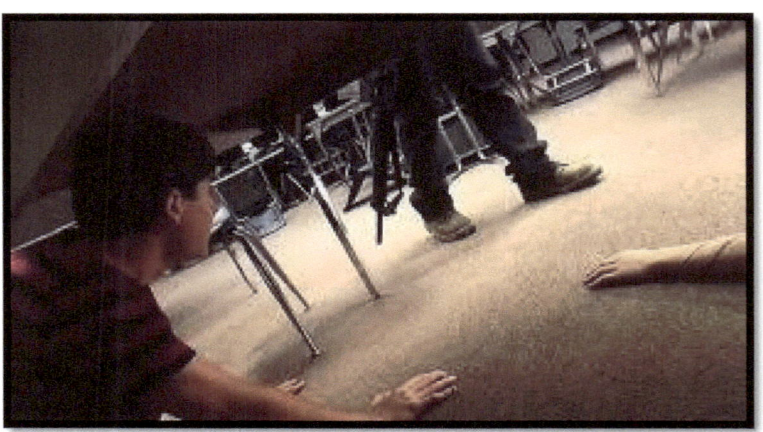

Hopefully you will never have to experience such a nightmare. But in the event you do, this is where your mental practice will translate into real-time decision making. If you can safely escape the location where the Active Shooter event is taking place, do it. Run away from the situation as quickly and quietly as you can.

Do not simply hide under a table or desk

If there is no way to escape the building without putting yourself directly in harm's way, then you will have to find another option. The next best one is to hide. But remember to hide with a purpose. Simply hiding under a table or desk has proven time and time again to be highly ineffective.

If you can find a good hiding location, don't be content to sit quietly, hoping that you will not be found. Find objects near you that could be used as defense weapons; staplers, keys, fire extinguishers, computers. Use anything that you can think of that could cause substantial harm to a person. Do not worry about the value of the property at this point. Property can be replaced, your life cannot.

Once you are hidden, with at least one weapon of opportunity in your hand, wait quietly. If the event concludes with you in your hiding location that is a great outcome. If you hear the attacker approaching your hiding location, remember that this is a violent encounter. Timid action is not an option when it comes to your safety. If the Active Shooter enters your area, get yourself prepared to launch a violent attack against this person that is taking lives.

16

Your goal at this point must be simple and wholehearted:

STOP THE THREAT!

This means that you must attack with as much energy and strength as you can muster. Do not let yourself hold back. Remember that in almost all Active Shooter incidents,  the suspect plans on their life ending, usually by their own hands. Do not be afraid of harming them.

 If you do not stop the threat when the Active Shooter enters your area, there is no reason they will not add you to their growing body count. This situation is no longer a "fair fight", it is time to fight as dirty as you can; gouging eyes, punching the throat, attacking the groin. There are no rules, only survival.

To stop the threat, you will need to, at a very minimum, dislodge the primary weapon from the shooter's hands. This may require knocking the suspect unconscious, maiming them, or even taking their life. Once the situation has come to this point, it is your life or theirs, there are no alternatives. This is a life or death battle.

Preparation ABC's
C – Conclusion

Conclusion – Prepare yourself for emergency personnel responses at the scene.

What should you expect once police respond to the scene? Remember that their **PRIMARY** objective is to end the violent encounter. They are not there to help you personally. Do not seek their assistance at this point. They are moving **toward** the sounds of gunfire; they will not help you to exit.

The situation is chaotic and law enforcement responders have no way of knowing who is a victim and who is a suspect. In some instances, Active Shooters have been known to pretend to be innocent bystanders. You can expect that they will demand to see your hands. Follow any directions given to you.

Do not ask emergency personnel to assist wounded victims. Again, their **FIRST** objective is to end the violent encounter, in order to limit the total number of victims. If they stopped to help all of the current victims, this would allow time for the suspect to add more victims to the growing number.

While you may already reasonably believe that the encounter has ended, emergency responders have protocols in place to ensure that threats no longer exist. Pending the satisfaction of these protocols, they will not be in a position to help the wounded. Until the threat has been completely neutralized, you must tend to your own wounds and the wounds of those around you.

It is important to remember the entire scene of an Active Shooter event will quickly transform into chaos and pandemonium. Do your best to remain calm. This will help first responders do their job, which will ultimately assist them in tending to your needs quicker.

Updating Your Loved Ones

Just as with any other tragic incident, when an Active Shooter incident takes place, others will want to know about your well-being.

DO NOT use your cell phone to text or call loved ones.

Past incidents have shown that when multiple people begin using their phones to contact others, it ties up the air waves of communication. This not only prevents necessary emergency calls from getting through, but ties up the communications for everybody.

DO USE social media as a way of updating others.

Facebook, Twitter, and other social media outlets can provide a great medium in getting your information out to others. This is because they do not use the same type of data as voice and text use. This keeps communication lines from being overwhelmed and bogged down.

DO NOT talk about the specifics of your location.

Example: "I am so scared right now. I'm hiding in the custodian closet so he doesn't find me."

DO USE information that reassures loved ones and helps emergency responders.

Example: "I'm scared, but I'm not hurt. I saw the shooter and he was wearing a yellow and red shirt, with a red hat."

DO NOT go to the scene of an incident where a loved one is trapped.

There is nothing you can do by being there. You will only create more traffic congestion for emergency vehicles that may need to get in or out of the scene. You will not be allowed into the immediate area. Your presence will only require the attention of more emergency personnel that could otherwise be focused on handling the situation.

DO USE rendezvous locations with your loved ones.

If possible, you should attempt to setup a location approximately 3-4 blocks away that can be used as a regrouping point. This could be either a pre-determined location, or you could use social media to communicate a meeting place with your loved one. Schools that have good Active Shooter protocols in place often have a location already determined.

Remember that this incident may be affecting you personally, but it is an event that is hurting the entire community. Acting on human nature and selfishly seeking your own interests often creates more unintentional chaos.

Preparing Your Family

While you may feel fairly confident in your own preparation for an Active Shooter incident, what about your family? It is imperative that your loved ones have plans in place just as you do.

For school age children, they often get training on what to *do* in such a situation. But they rarely receive training on

what to *expect*. You should review this information with your family so they have a better understanding of how they can protect themselves.

"Recognizing the increased active shooter threat and the swiftness with which active shooter incidents unfold, these study results support the importance of training and exercises— not only for law enforcement but also for citizens. It is important, too, that training and exercises include not only an understanding of the threats faced but also the risks and options available in active shooter incidents."

- FBI Study[1]

Advanced Preparation

Once you have taken the time to mentally prepare, you may discover that you also want some physical preparation. What additional steps can you take to prepare yourself for an Active Shooter incident?

Learn ways to discourage an Active Shooter: There are proven steps that you can take to greatly reduce the chances of your location becoming a target of an Active Shooter.

Create effective emergency escape plans: Just like with fires, there are usually a number of ways that you can escape from most buildings. Having these clearly defined is imperative to creating a successful escape plan.

Discover simple, effective techniques for quickly ending a violent encounter: Understanding your options can provide you with confidence, which is a huge factor in bringing an Active Shooter incident to a conclusion.

Train with personal defense tools: Carrying a tool for self-defense does not help you unless you train to properly use that tool under stress in an emergency situation.

Safe Insight has experienced, certified instructors that are happy to help assess your situation. We provide expert training in firearms and other personal defense tools. We also offer team-building courses that help groups locate weak areas at their location and create successful plans of action. Let us help you to create your safety plan.

"If you fail to plan, you are planning to fail!"

– Benjamin Franklin

WWW.SAFEINSIGHT.NET

For more information on Active Shooter Awareness or other courses we offer

Email:

Info@Safeinsight.net

Phone:

877-217-SAFE / 877-217-7233